The Dragon
Who Had the
Measles

Princess Petra had a huge pet dragon.
His name was Puffy McDuffy,
sometimes Puffy for short.

One day, he woke up with spots,
little red ones,
ALL over him—on his nose,
along his back, over his tum,
and right to the end of his tail.

4

The castle doctor was sent for immediately.
"Measles," he said.
"He must be put to bed,
kept warm,
and his eyes kept out of the light."

The maids put ten mattresses
down the corridor,
and they stitched thirty quilts together.
Princess Petra put Puffy to bed
with a hundred and fifty hot-water bottles
and gave him a pair of swish sunglasses.

But Puffy McDuffy was not very happy.

Aunt Fiddlesticks, the king's fairy aunt, flew in.
"I'll fix him," she said.
She waved her wand over poor old Puffy.
He gave an almighty sneeze
and blew Aunt Fiddlesticks away.

But he still had the measles.

"Poor Puffy!" said the queen.
"You need some fruit juice."
So she ordered fourteen gallons of fruit juice,
and Puffy drank it all up
through a big blue straw.

Princess Petra kept on refilling
the hot-water bottles.
She read him lots of stories.

At the end of the week, Puffy woke up.
The sun was shining.

"The spots have gone!" cried the queen.

"Disappeared!" cheered the maids.

"No more measles!" shouted the king.

Everyone was happy— Puffy McDuffy,
the doctor, the queen, the king,
Aunt Fiddlesticks, and the maids.

But Princess Petra was not happy.
Now *she* had the measles!